Artichoke Boy

Scott Mickelson

Boyds Mills Press
Honesdale, Pennsylvania

This is the story of Artichoke Boy,
whose life was filled with artichoke joy.

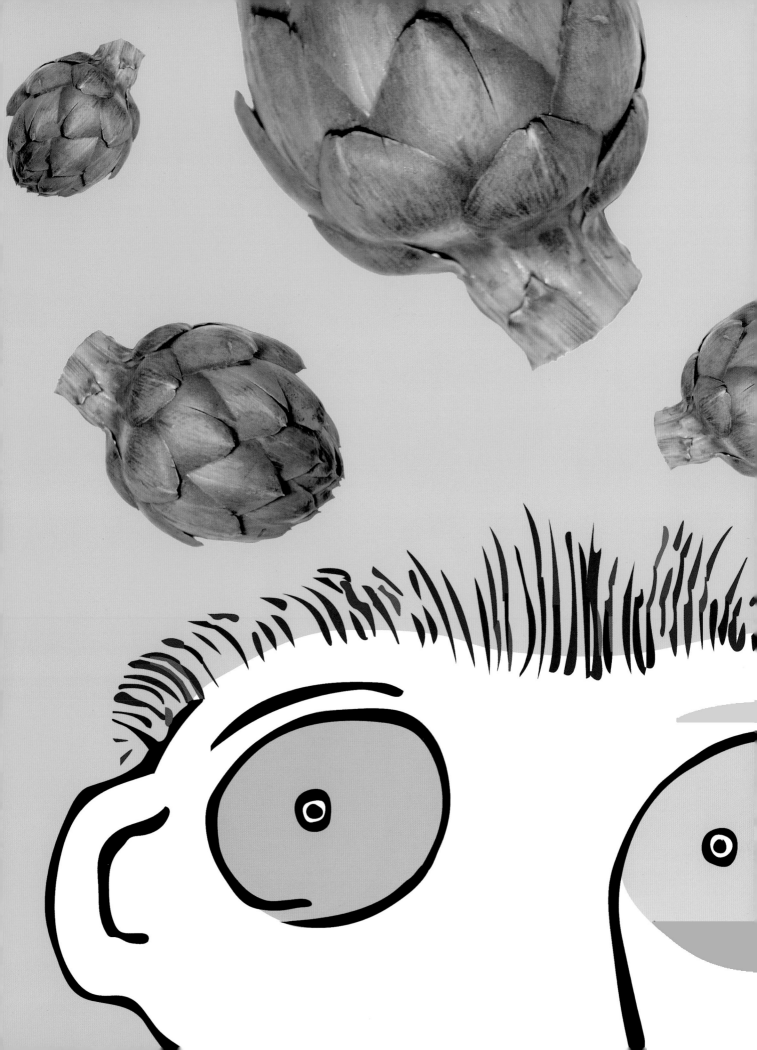

He had artichoke fingers
and an artichoke nose ...

artichoke ears . . .

and wore artichoke clothes.

He had artichoke elbows and artichoke knees …

and make-believe friends—

the artichoke bees.

He had artichoke eyeballs

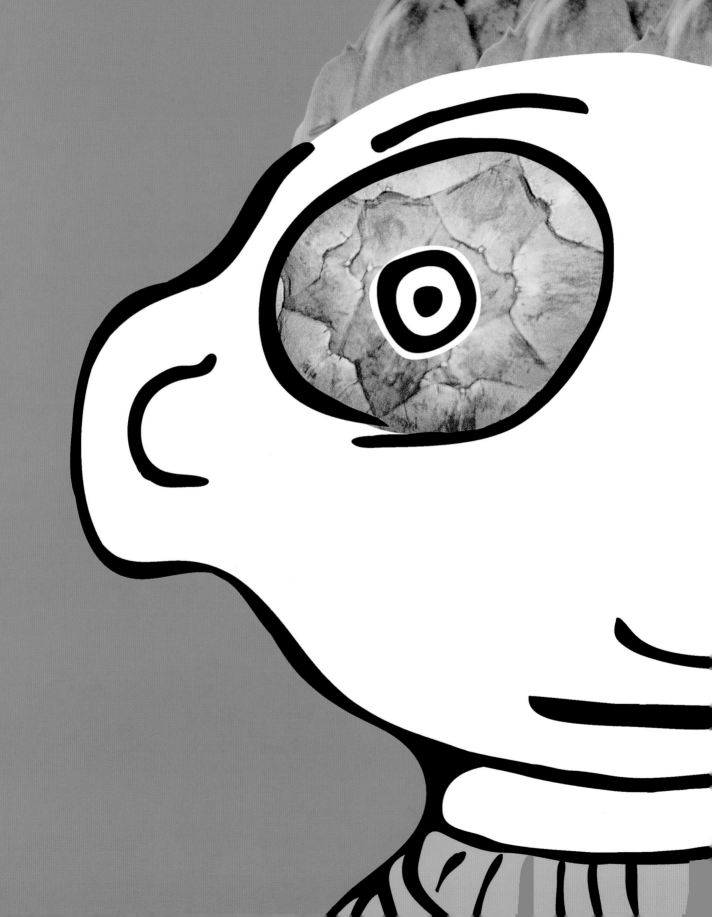

and artichoke hair . . .

and was proud of his artichoke derriere.

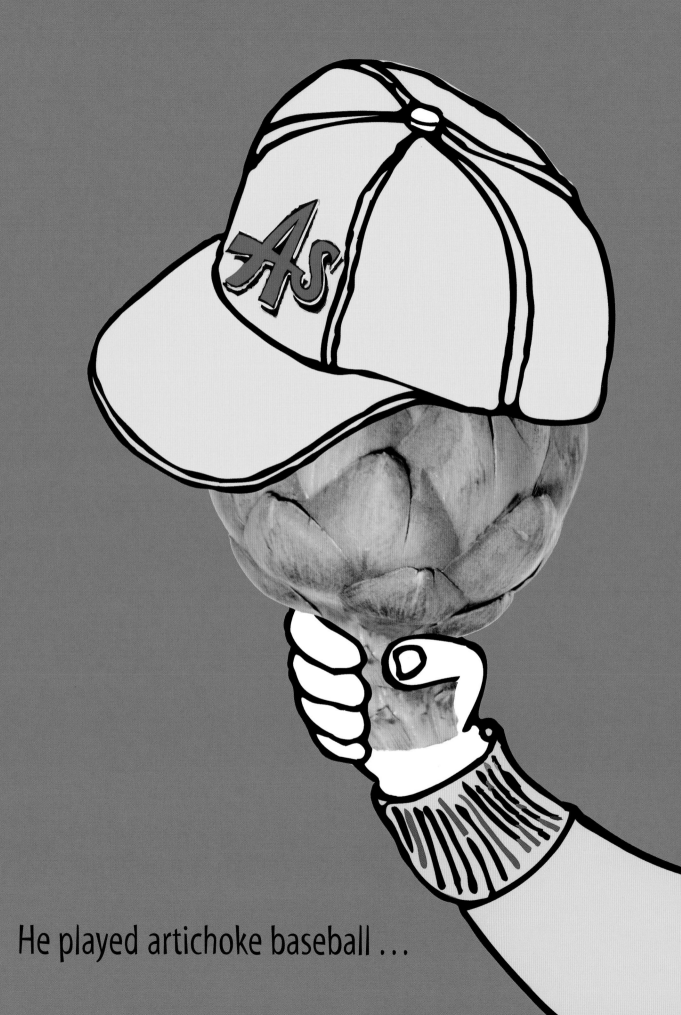

He played artichoke baseball . . .

rode an artichoke sled,

and every night slept in his artichoke bed.

He had an artichoke toothbrush

and took artichoke baths . . .

and on Halloween night wore an artichoke mask.

He had an artichoke fish and a sister named Kelly ...

who couldn't zip her coat
over her artichoke belly!

His mother wore an
artichoke on her head
as a hat and
sitting on her lap was
an artichoke cat.

His father drove an artichoke on his way to work
and had pictures of artichokes

on his tie and his shirt.

They had artichoke dinners ...

and made artichoke drinks,

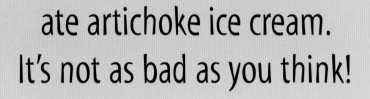

ate artichoke ice cream.
It's not as bad as you think!

Artichoke Boy loved artichokes

spring, summer, winter, and fall.

But it was his artichoke family
that he loved most of all.

Thanks to my wife, Deborah,
and my little artichoke girl, Sadie

Boyds Mills Press, Inc.
815 Church Street
Honesdale, Pennsylvania 18431
Printed in China

CIP data is available

First edition
The text of this book is set in 30-point Myriad Tilt.
The illustrations are done in mixed media.

10 9 8 7 6 5 4 3 2 1